Katie Clemons
LET'S CELEBRATE YOU

T0063684

OUR

PRAYER

JOURNAL

CELEBRATING OUR
CHRISTIAN FAITH TOGETHER

sourcebooks
eXplore

TO GRANDMA MARIE
I'M BETTER BECAUSE OF HER RESOLVE IN THE POWER
OF PRAYER AND UNRELENTING LOVE FOR US ALL.

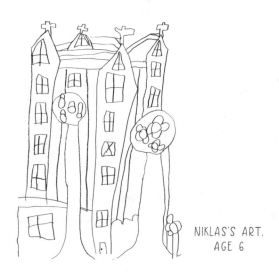

NIKLAS'S ART.
AGE 6

Copyright © 2020 by Katie Clemons LLC
Cover and internal design © 2020 by Sourcebooks
Cover and internal illustrations by Maryn Arreguín and Katie Clemons LLC (page 2)

Sourcebooks and the colophon are registered trademarks of Sourcebooks.

All rights reserved.

Published by Sourcebooks eXplore, an imprint of Sourcebooks Kids
P.O. Box 4410, Naperville, Illinois 60567-4410
(630) 961-3900
sourcebookskids.com

Source of Production: Versa Press, East Peoria, Illinois, USA
Date of Production: September 2020
Run Number: 5019412

Printed and bound in the United States of America.
VP 10 9 8 7 6 5 4 3 2 1

LET'S NOTICE LIFE'S BLESSINGS

I COULDN'T SPOT a single empty hand when we recited The Lord's Prayer at church that chilly winter morning. Everyone reached out to people beside them. They stretched across aisles and rows to connect with friends and strangers alike. If someone couldn't rise, a row of arms elongated toward them. Three hands might come together. And if my baby sister were willing, a welcoming finger presented itself for her to wrap her chubby fingers around it.

Then we all began: "Our Father who art in heaven, hallowed be thy Name..."

The room felt warm with our words, and so did my heart. Coming together to pray made me feel connected, like I was a kid invited into something big and beautiful, something much greater than myself. I held my arms high and recited every word.

And then, like always, our prayer came to an end. My congregation unclasped hands. They dropped their arms and shifted back to their respective spots as the service continued.

Except my mom. She kept holding my hand. I didn't know why she did that. I just knew I didn't want her to let go.

That was when everything changed. I felt her squeeze my hand one...two...three times.

I looked up at her and whispered, "What's that for?"

She smiled and triple squeezed my hand again in rhythm with her words. "It means I...love...you, Katie."

Maybe my mom felt like her impulse wasn't anything special at first. But after that moment, I remember seeking her side at church more often. I would reach for her hand to share our secret squeeze as we went about our days. Whenever I felt scared or lacked confidence, I could always feel that reminder of her affection.

Now that I'm a parent, I recognize how precious those simple interactions with my mom were, and I'm certain that this child you love craves more opportunities to connect with you too.

As parents and caring adults, we've got so many expectations and to-do lists that keep us hustling. But I also know that none of us wants to miss those precious moments when a child's hand rests in ours or their eyes shine with love.

Kids watch how adults they love respond to the world. When you love thy neighbor, seek and offer forgiveness, and exhibit gestures of everyday kindness, you offer an example they can aspire to. They observe how you deal with perceived failures calmly and practice your faith. Then they strive to model the same behavior.

Over the years, I've discovered that keeping a journal is both the easiest and most powerful way for me to become more receptive to the blessings in my life, and I relish witnessing how journaling does that for other people. When we put our pen to paper, we instinctively begin to recognize, celebrate, and share God's gifts.

This journal is my invitation for you and a child you love to openly express your faith and discuss timely topics in your lives—conversations and questions that may never surface at the dinner table or in church.

As you answer prompts that make you chuckle or that invite conversations on deeper issues, you both discover your commonalities and varied views. Some prompts challenge you to roll up your sleeves and do something, while others invite introspection. An occasional prompt will help kids openly communicate their faith questions. As you work through the pages, you'll discover that writing together enables you to nurture an intimate, more fulfilling relationship with both each other and God.

These days when I return to my Montana hometown and my kids and I step into that same warm and welcoming church, I still try to stand beside my mom. I raise my arms during The Lord's Prayer. Then when everyone begins to unfold our chain of hands, I hang onto my mom. I feel her soft, wrinkled skin against mine, and we both begin to squeeze *I...love...you.*

Let this journal be a beacon of light for you and this child you love. These five guideposts will help you get the most from your storycatching time together.

1. BEGIN ON ANY PAGE.

You don't have to use the pages in this journal chronologically. Both of you can respond to any prompt you're drawn to whenever you want. Answer the questions together while you pray or sip hot chocolate, or pass the book back and forth, making entries in turn.

Your child's stories go on pages that begin "Dear Child" or "I Write." Correlating "My Question for You" and "You Write" pages provide you with an opportunity to reply or launch another conversation. When you see a "My Question for You" page, imagine your child prompting you: "Hey Adult-I-Love, this is my question for you…" They're launching the conversation and awaiting your reply below. Then intermixed throughout the book are spaces to doodle, write, and stick keepsakes in together. Photographs are completely optional.

2. EMBRACE IMPERFECTION.

This side of heaven, we all have flaws. God doesn't look at you and see missteps; God cherishes love. Over the years, I've discovered that letting your pen and mind wander imperfectly through the pages often results in the best prayers and greatest connections.

My own journals are sprinkled with crossed-out words, arrows that reroute sentences around the paper, and at least half a dozen creative ways to spell *crucifixion*. But I keep journaling, and I want you to as well, because I have learned that praying with pen to paper is infinitely more powerful than any empty page.

3. BECOME AN ENGAGED LISTENER.

The real joy in shared journaling begins when you pause from your busy day to read what your child has written. As you look at their words, try to understand what they're really communicating. Do they want you to change something or explain something? Or do they just need you to lend an ear or help them pray as they navigate through things?

Sharing this journal gives you both a peek inside one another's heads and relationship with God. Some entries address things you already know. Others can reveal emotions, entire stories, or prayer requests you weren't aware of—from either of you. You can write a response immediately, or you can walk away to pray and reflect for a while.

4. PLAY.

This journal is a home for words, and it's also a place to play! Add colorful emojis. Trace your hands. Doodle colorful speech bubbles and arrows. Underline words with different pens. Jot giant AMENS everywhere. Add gathered mementos and decorate with stickers. Draw pictures or snap photographs and adhere them with glue or double-sided tape. Above all, enjoy the process.

5. GO BEYOND THESE PAGES.

Your journaling experience only begins in this book. You're warmly welcome to explore my exclusive *Our Prayer Journal* resources including more fun prayer projects, easy Saturday-nightin faith games, and journaling jokes that'll have both of you rolling with laughter.

KATIECLEMONS.COM/A/GM66

I'd love to hear how your journal is coming together. Please write to me at **howdy@katieclemons.com** (I answer all my mail) or join me on social media **@katierclemons**, **#katieclemonsjournals**, and **#ourprayerjournal**.

Imagine opening this journal in ten or twenty years or giving it to your grown child. You'll see pages filled with stories and perspectives, pictures, youthful penmanship recording prayers you haven't thought about in years, and best of all...reminders of how much your lives have been blessed.

Peace be with you, and... Let's celebrate your story!

THE GREATEST GIFT GOD GIVES IS LOVE

HERE'S A PHOTOGRAPH OR DRAWING OF

YOU & ME

HELLO TODAY!

OUR FULL NAMES ARE

_____

_____

WE CALL EACH OTHER

_____

_____

WE'RE _____ AND _____ YEARS OLD.

WE'RE GRATEFUL FOR EACH OTHER BECAUSE

_____

_____

LET'S START THIS JOURNAL!

DATE: _____

OUR JOURNAL GUIDELINES

1. IS OUR JOURNAL TOP SECRET OR CAN ANYONE ELSE LOOK INSIDE?

_____

_____

2. IF SOMEONE FINDS THIS JOURNAL, THEY SHOULD

☐ RETURN IT

☐ COMPLETE IT

☐ DESTROY IT

☐ DROP IT OFF AT THIS CHURCH: _____

_____

☐ HIDE IT IN _____

☐ DONATE IT TO THE LOCAL ARCHIVES

☐ _____

3. DO WE HAVE TO ANSWER PROMPTS IN NUMERICAL ORDER?   ☐ YES   ☐ NO

4. OUR TOP FOCUS(ES) IN THIS JOURNAL WILL BE TO

☐ EXPRESS OUR THOUGHTS

☐ GROW CLOSER TO GOD

☐ CAPTURE MEMORIES

☐ CONNECT WITH ONE ANOTHER

☐ USE PERFECT GRAMMAR

☐ PRAY TOGETHER

☐ REFLECT ON GRATITUDE

☐ SKIP OUR RESPONSIBILITIES SUCH AS _____

_____

_____ IN ORDER TO WRITE

☐ _____

☐ _____

5. HOW MUCH TIME DO WE HAVE TO WRITE BEFORE PASSING OUR JOURNAL BACK TO EACH OTHER?

_____

_____

_____

6. WHAT COULD WE DO IF WE NEED MORE SPACE TO WRITE? _____

_____

_____

_____

7. IS THERE A SPECIFIC DATE WHEN THIS JOURNAL MUST BE COMPLETE? _____

_____

_____

_____

8. HOW DO WE PASS OUR JOURNAL BACK AND FORTH?

_____

_____

_____

_____

9. HOW SHOULD WE TELL EACH OTHER WHICH PAGE TO
TURN TO? _____

_____

_____

_____

10. HOW CAN WE COMMUNICATE WHEN WE NEED AN
URGENT RESPONSE? _____

_____

_____

_____

11. ARE THERE OTHER GUIDELINES WE SHOULD
ESTABLISH FOR OUR JOURNAL? _____

_____

_____

_____

DEAR CHILD,

WHAT'S SOMETHING GOD HAS GIVEN YOU THAT MAKES YOU HAPPY?

MY QUESTION FOR YOU,

WHAT'S SOMETHING GOD HAS GIVEN
YOU THAT MAKES YOU HAPPY?

YOU & ME

OUR HOPEFUL FACES

YOU

ME

OUR GIVE-ME-A-HUGE-HUG FACES

YOU

ME

OUR I'M-EXPLODING-WITH-JOY FACES

YOU

ME

WE WRITE

I WRITE

WAYS I FEEL GOD IN MY LIFE THIS WEEK

YOU WRITE

WAYS I FEEL GOD IN MY LIFE THIS WEEK

DEAR CHILD,

WHAT DO YOU THINK IT MEANS TO BE A CHRISTIAN?

HOW DO YOU TRY TO BE CHRISTLIKE IN YOUR DAILY LIFE?

MY QUESTION FOR YOU,

WHAT DO YOU THINK IT MEANS TO BE A CHRISTIAN?

HOW DO YOU TRY TO BE CHRISTLIKE IN YOUR DAILY LIFE?

DEAR CHILD,

WHAT KIND OF LIFE DO YOU THINK
GOD WANTS YOU TO LIVE?

HOW DOES THAT COME EASILY TO YOU?

HOW IS IT CHALLENGING?

MY QUESTION FOR YOU,

WHAT DO YOU THINK ABOUT WHAT I WROTE?

WHAT KIND OF LIFE DO YOU THINK
GOD WANTS YOU TO LIVE?

HOW DOES THAT COME EASILY TO YOU?
AND HOW IS IT CHALLENGING?

YOU WRITE

CHILD, I REALLY ADMIRE HOW YOU LOVE LIKE JESUS TAUGHT US TO WHEN YOU

1.

2.

3.

I THINK GOD HAS BLESSED YOU WITH

YOU'RE REALLY GOOD AT

HERE'S A PICTURE OF YOU,

MY _____!

I WRITE

I REALLY ADMIRE HOW YOU LOVE LIKE JESUS TAUGHT US TO WHEN YOU

1.

2.

3.

I THINK GOD HAS BLESSED YOU WITH

YOU'RE REALLY GOOD AT

CHILD WRITES

HERE'S A PICTURE OF YOU,
MY _____!

I WRITE
TODAY I'M NOTICING

THE SOUND OF

THE SMELL OF

THE SIGHT OF

THE FEEL OF

THE TASTE OF

CHILD WRITES

 THANK YOU, GOD!

YOU WRITE

TODAY I'M NOTICING

THE SOUND OF

THE SMELL OF

THE SIGHT OF

THE FEEL OF

THE TASTE OF

THANK YOU, GOD! ♡

DEAR CHILD,

TELL ME ABOUT A TIME WHEN GOD ANSWERED YOUR PRAYER

HOW DID IT MAKE YOU FEEL?

WHY DO YOU THINK IT'S IMPORTANT TO TURN TO GOD WITH OUR PRAYERS?

MY QUESTION FOR YOU,

TELL ME ABOUT A TIME WHEN GOD ANSWERED YOUR PRAYER

HOW DID IT MAKE YOU FEEL?

WHY DO YOU THINK IT'S IMPORTANT TO TURN TO GOD WITH OUR PRAYERS?

DEAR CHILD,

TELL ME ABOUT A TIME WHEN GOD DIDN'T ANSWER
YOUR PRAYER THE WAY YOU'D ENVISIONED

WHY DO YOU THINK GOD DID THAT?

MY QUESTION FOR YOU,

WHAT DO YOU THINK ABOUT WHAT I WROTE?

TELL ME ABOUT A TIME WHEN GOD DIDN'T ANSWER
YOUR PRAYER THE WAY YOU'D ENVISIONED

WHY DO YOU THINK GOD DID THAT?

I WRITE

I BELIEVE HEAVEN

SOUNDS LIKE

TASTES LIKE

LOOKS LIKE

SMELLS LIKE

FEELS LIKE

DATE

I BELIEVE HEAVEN

SOUNDS LIKE

TASTES LIKE

LOOKS LIKE

SMELLS LIKE

FEELS LIKE

DEAR CHILD,

IF YOU WERE SHOWING SOMEONE HOW TO PRAY FOR THE FIRST TIME, WHAT WOULD YOU TEACH THEM?

MY QUESTION FOR YOU,

IF YOU WERE SHOWING SOMEONE
HOW TO PRAY FOR THE FIRST TIME,
WHAT WOULD YOU TEACH THEM?

I WRITE

MY FAMILY

MY COUNTRY

TODAY I PRAY FOR

MY COMMUNITY

MY HOME

YOU WRITE

MY FAMILY

MY COUNTRY

TODAY I PRAY FOR

MY COMMUNITY

MY HOME

I WRITE

MY FAVORITE PRAYER IS

I REALLY LIKE THE WORDS IN THIS PART

I REPEAT THIS PRAYER WHEN

IT MAKES ME FEEL

I THINK IT'S HELPFUL TO MEMORIZE
SPECIFIC PRAYERS BECAUSE

YOU WRITE

MY FAVORITE PRAYER IS

I REALLY LIKE THE WORDS IN THIS PART

I REPEAT THIS PRAYER WHEN

IT MAKES ME FEEL

I THINK IT'S HELPFUL TO MEMORIZE
SPECIFIC PRAYERS BECAUSE

I WRITE

MY FAVORITE SPOT TO PRAY AT HOME

YOU WRITE

MY FAVORITE SPOT TO PRAY AT HOME

WE WRITE

YOU & ME

WE TREASURE THIS SONG

YOU

ME

WE ENJOY THIS BOOK OR MAGAZINE

YOU

ME

WE LOVE THIS MOVIE OR SHOW

YOU

ME

DEAR CHILD,

SHOW ME A
PICTURE OF
A HOBBY
YOU LOVE

WHEN YOU'RE DOING THIS ACTIVITY, HOW DOES
IT MAKE YOU FEEL ABOUT YOURSELF?

CAN YOU FEEL GOD'S PRESENCE IN YOUR PASSION?

IT GETS ☆☆☆☆☆ STARS!

44   **CHILD** WRITES

MY QUESTION FOR YOU,

SHOW ME A
PICTURE OF
A HOBBY
YOU LOVE

WHEN YOU'RE DOING THIS ACTIVITY, HOW DOES
IT MAKE YOU FEEL ABOUT YOURSELF?

CAN YOU FEEL GOD'S PRESENCE IN YOUR PASSION?

IT GETS ☆☆☆☆☆ STARS!

I WRITE

I CAN SEE GOD'S PRESENCE THROUGHOUT THE YEAR

SPRING

SUMMER

FALL

WINTER

I CAN SEE GOD'S PRESENCE THROUGHOUT THE YEAR

SPRING

SUMMER

FALL

WINTER

DEAR CHILD,

DO YOU BELIEVE GOD HAS A PLAN FOR YOU?

WHAT'S SOMETHING GOD HAS
ALREADY GUIDED YOU THROUGH?

WHAT'S SOMETHING YOU HOPE YOU CAN
EXPERIENCE WITH OUR LORD'S HELP?

MY QUESTION FOR YOU,

WHAT DO YOU THINK ABOUT WHAT I WROTE?

DO YOU BELIEVE GOD HAS A PLAN FOR YOU?

WHAT'S SOMETHING GOD HAS
ALREADY GUIDED YOU THROUGH?

WHAT'S SOMETHING YOU HOPE YOU CAN
EXPERIENCE WITH OUR LORD'S HELP?

I WRITE

WHEN I PRAY BY MYSELF,

MY HANDS ARE

MY VOICE IS

MY BODY IS

YOU WRITE

WHEN I PRAY BY MYSELF,

MY HANDS ARE

MY VOICE IS

MY BODY IS

WE WRITE

WHEN WE PRAY TOGETHER,

OUR HANDS ARE

OUR VOICES ARE

OUR BODIES ARE

YOU & ME

WE ALWAYS ENJOY

TIME ALONE TO

YOU

ME

TIME TOGETHER TO

YOU

ME

TIME WITH GOD TO

YOU

ME

WE WRITE   55

YOU & ME

GIFTS GOD HAS GIVEN US

I WRITE

YOU WRITE

WE WRITE

DEAR CHILD,

DO YOU HAVE ANY QUESTIONS I COULD
HELP YOU ANSWER ABOUT OUR FAITH?

MY ANSWER FOR YOU,

HERE'S WHAT I KNOW ABOUT OUR FAITH

DEAR CHILD,

DO YOU HAVE A QUESTION I COULD
HELP YOU ANSWER ABOUT

GOD

CHURCH

THE BIBLE

JESUS

MARY

SIN

YOU PICK!

MY ANSWER FOR YOU,

HERE'S WHAT I BELIEVE

DEAR CHILD,

WHAT ARE THREE THINGS YOU'D LIKE TO ACHIEVE?

1.

2.

3.

HOW DO YOU THINK GOD CAN GUIDE YOU?

WHAT'S A RECENT ACCOMPLISHMENT YOU'RE PROUD OF?

HOW DO YOU BELIEVE GOD HELPED YOU?

CHILD WRITES

MY QUESTION FOR YOU,

WHAT DO YOU THINK ABOUT WHAT I WROTE?

WHAT'S SOMETHING YOU'D LIKE TO ACHIEVE?

HOW DO YOU THINK GOD CAN GUIDE YOU?

WHAT'S A RECENT ACCOMPLISHMENT YOU'RE PROUD OF?
AND HOW DO YOU BELIEVE GOD HELPED YOU?

I WRITE

MY TYPICAL SABBATH DAY

6:00 _____

7:00 _____

8:00 _____

9:00 _____

10:00 _____

11:00 _____

NOON _____

1:00 _____

2:00 _____

3:00 _____

4:00 _____

5:00 _____

6:00 _____

7:00 _____

8:00 _____

9:00 _____

10:00 _____

YOU WRITE

MY TYPICAL SABBATH DAY

6:00 ....

7:00 ....

8:00 ....

9:00 ....

10:00 ....

11:00 ....

NOON ....

1:00 ....

2:00 ....

3:00 ....

4:00 ....

5:00 ....

6:00 ....

7:00 ....

8:00 ....

9:00 ....

10:00 ....

WE ALWAYS ENJOY

YOU & ME

THIS TRADITION

YOU

ME

THIS HOLIDAY

YOU

ME

THIS CHRISTIAN CUSTOM

YOU

ME

WE WRITE

YOU & ME

THIS IS OUR FAMILY AT MEALTIME

THIS IS HOW WE SAY GRACE

BREAKING BREAD TOGETHER MAKES US FEEL

I WRITE
PEOPLE WHO'VE INSPIRED MY FAITH JOURNEY

YOU WRITE

PEOPLE WHO'VE INSPIRED MY FAITH JOURNEY

CHRISTLIKE WORDS AND GESTURES WE'VE WITNESSED RECENTLY

DATE

69

DEAR CHILD,

HOW DO YOU KNOW GOD'S LISTENING?

MY QUESTION FOR YOU,

HOW DO YOU KNOW GOD'S LISTENING?

I WRITE

TODAY, I

FEEL

HEAR

SMELL

BELIEVE

WORRY

LOVE

PRAY

YOU WRITE

TODAY, I

FEEL

HEAR

SMELL

BELIEVE

WORRY

LOVE

PRAY

DEAR CHILD,

TELL ME ABOUT A TIME WHEN A STRANGER
HELPED YOU WITH SOMETHING.

HOW DID IT MAKE YOU FEEL?

WHY DO YOU THINK THEY DID IT?

MY QUESTION FOR YOU,

WHAT DO YOU THINK ABOUT WHAT I WROTE?

TELL ME ABOUT A TIME WHEN A STRANGER
HELPED YOU WITH SOMETHING.

HOW DID IT MAKE YOU FEEL?
AND WHY DO YOU THINK THEY DID IT?

I WRITE
TODAY, I PRAY FOR

THIS FRIEND

THIS MENTOR

THIS NEIGHBOR

THIS FAMILY MEMBER

THIS LEADER

YOU WRITE

TODAY, I PRAY FOR

THIS FRIEND

THIS MENTOR

THIS NEIGHBOR

THIS FAMILY MEMBER

THIS LEADER

I WRITE

HERE'S SOME SCRIPTURE OR A QUOTE I WANT
TO INCLUDE IN OUR JOURNAL

I'M INCLUDING IT HERE BECAUSE

YOU WRITE

HERE'S SOME SCRIPTURE OR A QUOTE I WANT TO INCLUDE IN OUR JOURNAL

I'M INCLUDING IT HERE BECAUSE

I WRITE

I CAN SEE GOD'S WORK THROUGHOUT THE DAY

MORNING

AFTERNOON

EVENING

NIGHT

CHILD WRITES

YOU WRITE

I CAN SEE GOD'S WORK THROUGHOUT THE DAY

MORNING

AFTERNOON

EVENING

NIGHT

DEAR CHILD,

TELL ME ABOUT SOMEONE YOU ADMIRE

HOW DOES THIS PERSON LIVE IN A CHRISTLIKE WAY?

WHY DOES THIS PERSON INSPIRE YOU SO MUCH?

ADD AN INSPIRATIONAL QUOTE OR PASSAGE

HOW IS OUR COMMUNITY OR WORLD A
BETTER PLACE BECAUSE OF THIS PERSON?

TELL ME ABOUT AN OBSTACLE THIS PERSON
HAD TO OVERCOME

HOW DO YOU THINK GOD GUIDED THEM?

KEEP GOING

DO YOU THINK THIS PERSON EVER MADE
A MISTAKE OR FELT LIKE THEY'D FAILED?
WHY DO YOU THINK THEY KEPT GOING?

DESCRIBE HOW YOU'RE SIMILAR TO THIS PERSON

1.

2.

3.

HOW COULD YOU
BE MORE LIKE
THIS PERSON?

FUTURE ME, AGE _____

CHILD WRITES

MY QUESTION FOR YOU,

WHAT ARE YOUR THOUGHTS ON WHAT
I WROTE ABOUT THE PERSON I ADMIRE?

WHICH TRAITS DO I SHARE WITH THEM?

1.

2.

3.

I WRITE

I SEE GOD WHEN

YOU WRITE

I SEE GOD WHEN

WE WRITE

YOU & ME

DEAR GOD, TODAY WE PRAY FOR THOSE IN NEED, ESPECIALLY THOSE WHO ARE

SUFFERING

SICK

LONELY

POOR

UNEMPLOYED

DISTRESSED

NEGLECTED

PERSECUTED

....

BECAUSE

_____

_____

PLEASE COMFORT AND HEAL THEM WITH

_____

_____

PLEASE GUIDE THEM WITH

_____

_____

AMEN.

DEAR CHILD,

I HAVE A QUESTION FOR YOU

?

MY QUESTION FOR YOU,

CHILD WRITES QUESTION HERE

?

I WRITE

DEAR GOD,
THANK YOU FOR GIVING ME

THE WISDOM TO

_____

THE HEALTH TO

_____

THE CONFIDENCE TO

_____

A COMMUNITY THAT

_____

THE STRENGTH TO

_____

THE GUIDANCE TO

_____

THE PATIENCE TO

_____

FAITHFULNESS WHEN

_____

AMEN.

YOU WRITE

DEAR GOD,
THANK YOU FOR GIVING ME

THE WISDOM TO

_____

THE HEALTH TO

_____

THE CONFIDENCE TO

_____

A COMMUNITY THAT

_____

THE STRENGTH TO

_____

THE GUIDANCE TO

_____

THE PATIENCE TO

_____

FAITHFULNESS WHEN

_____

AMEN.

YOU & ME

HOW WE MODEL GOD'S LOVE TOWARD

OUR FAMILY

OUR FRIENDS

EACH OTHER

THOSE IN NEED

STRANGERS

OUR TEACHERS, ROLE MODELS, OR MENTORS

OURSELVES

WE WRITE

YOU & ME

SOMETHING WE CAN

HELP PEOPLE WE LOVE WITH

YOU

ME

GIVE TO STRANGERS

YOU

ME

REJOICE BECAUSE GOD HAS GIVEN US ALL

YOU

ME

I WRITE

AT CHRISTMAS, MY HOUSE

SMELLS LIKE _____

TASTES LIKE _____

LOOKS LIKE _____

SOUNDS LIKE _____

FEELS LIKE _____

MY CHURCH

SMELLS LIKE _____

TASTES LIKE _____

LOOKS LIKE _____

SOUNDS LIKE _____

FEELS LIKE _____

CHILD WRITES

MY FAVORITE CHRISTMAS SONG IS

_____

I LOVE THESE LYRICS _____

_____

I RELISH THIS TRADITION _____

_____

I TRY TO MAKE THE HOLIDAY NICER FOR PEOPLE I
LOVE BY_____

_____

I TRY TO MAKE IT A NICER CELEBRATION FOR THOSE
IN NEED BY_____

_____

I THINK THAT BEING A CHRISTIAN AT
CHRISTMASTIME MEANS _____

_____

MY FAVORITE PART OF THE CHRISTMAS STORY IS

_____

IF I COULD HAVE GIVEN JESUS A GIFT AT THE
MANGER, IT WOULD HAVE BEEN _____

_____

YOU WRITE

AT CHRISTMAS, MY HOUSE

SMELLS LIKE _____

TASTES LIKE _____

LOOKS LIKE _____

SOUNDS LIKE _____

FEELS LIKE _____

MY CHURCH

SMELLS LIKE _____

TASTES LIKE _____

LOOKS LIKE _____

SOUNDS LIKE _____

FEELS LIKE _____

ADULT WRITES

MY FAVORITE CHRISTMAS SONG IS

_____

I LOVE THESE LYRICS _____

_____

I RELISH THIS TRADITION _____

_____

I TRY TO MAKE THE HOLIDAY NICER FOR PEOPLE I
LOVE BY_____

_____

I TRY TO MAKE IT A NICER CELEBRATION FOR THOSE
IN NEED BY_____

_____

I THINK THAT BEING A CHRISTIAN AT
CHRISTMASTIME MEANS _____

_____

MY FAVORITE PART OF THE CHRISTMAS STORY IS

_____

IF I COULD HAVE GIVEN JESUS A GIFT AT THE
MANGER, IT WOULD HAVE BEEN _____

_____

GLORIA

I WRITE

AT THE STABLE, I IMAGINE
JOSEPH AND MARY MUST HAVE

FELT

HEARD

SMELLED

WORRIED

LOVED

PRAYED

TRUSTED

BELIEVED

HOPED

THIS MAKES ME FEEL _____

_____

GLORIA

YOU WRITE

AT THE STABLE, I IMAGINE
JOSEPH AND MARY MUST HAVE

FELT

HEARD

SMELLED

WORRIED

LOVED

PRAYED

TRUSTED

BELIEVED

HOPED

THIS MAKES ME FEEL _____

_____

YOU & ME

A PRAYER OF
THANKSGIVING
WE CAN SAY ON A GREAT DAY

YOU

ME

WE WRITE

A PRAYER OF
THANKSGIVING
WE CAN SAY ON A DIFFICULT DAY

YOU
& ME

YOU

ME

MY QUESTION FOR YOU,

DO YOU REMEMBER A TEMPTATION OR SIN THAT
YOU STRUGGLED WITH WHEN YOU WERE MY AGE?

HOW DID YOU NAVIGATE THROUGH IT?

HOW HAS OVERCOMING IT HELPED YOU
BE A BETTER PERSON TODAY?

DEAR CHILD,

WHAT TEMPTATION OR SIN ARE YOU
STRUGGLING WITH RIGHT NOW?

IS THERE A WAY I CAN HELP YOU?

HOW IS GOD GUIDING YOU?

HOW WE MODEL
GOD'S LOVE TOWARD

THE ENVIRONMENT

OUR HOMES

PETS AROUND US

WILD ANIMALS

PLANTS

OUR FAVORITE THINGS

WE PICK!

WE WRITE

I WRITE

WAYS GOD HAS PROVIDED FOR ME THIS WEEK

1.

2.

3.

4.

YOU WRITE

WAYS GOD HAS PROVIDED FOR ME THIS WEEK

1.

2.

3.

4.

DEAR CHILD,

TELL ME ABOUT SOMETHING THAT MAKES YOU WORRY

WHY DO YOU THINK IT BOTHERS YOU SO MUCH?

DO YOU HAVE ANY IDEAS ON HOW YOU
COULD EASE YOUR CONCERNS?

ARE THERE WAYS YOU'D LIKE ME TO HELP?

HOW DO YOU KNOW GOD IS AIDING
YOU WITH YOUR TROUBLES?

WRITE A PRAYER ASKING FOR GOD'S STRENGTH

MY QUESTION FOR YOU,

WHAT ARE YOUR THOUGHTS ON WHAT WORRIES ME?

DO YOU HAVE ANY IDEAS ON HOW I COULD
WORRY LESS? MAYBE WITH YOUR HELP?

WHAT DO YOU DO WHEN SOMETHING CONCERNS YOU?

WHAT DO YOU ALWAYS TELL ME?

HOW HAVE YOU SEEN GOD GUIDING ME
THROUGH MY TROUBLES?

WILL YOU WRITE A PRAYER FOR ME?

DEAR CHILD,

DO YOU KNOW ANYONE WHO ISN'T CHRISTIAN?

HOW DO YOU THINK WE SHOULD TREAT PEOPLE
WHOSE FAITH IS DIFFERENT FROM OURS?

DO THE PEOPLE YOU KNOW HAVE CUSTOMS OR
HOLIDAYS THAT WE DON'T CELEBRATE?

HOW DO YOU BELIEVE WE SHOULD BEHAVE
TOWARD THEIR CUSTOMS OR HOLIDAYS?

HAVE YOU EVER SEEN CHRISTIANS BEHAVING
DIFFERENTLY? HOW DOES IT MAKE YOU FEEL?

DO YOU KNOW ANYONE WHO ISN'T CHRISTIAN?

HOW DO YOU THINK WE SHOULD TREAT PEOPLE WHOSE FAITH IS DIFFERENT FROM OURS?

DO THE PEOPLE YOU KNOW HAVE CUSTOMS OR HOLIDAYS THAT WE DON'T CELEBRATE?

HOW DO YOU BELIEVE WE SHOULD BEHAVE TOWARD THEIR CUSTOMS OR HOLIDAYS?

HAVE YOU EVER SEEN CHRISTIANS BEHAVING DIFFERENTLY? HOW DOES IT MAKE YOU FEEL?

I WRITE

PEOPLE WHO LOVE AND APPRECIATE ME

PEOPLE I LOVE AND APPRECIATE

PEOPLE WHO LOVE AND APPRECIATE ME

PEOPLE I LOVE AND APPRECIATE

DEAR CHILD,

DO YOU THINK IT'S IMPORTANT TO ATTEND CHURCH?

WHAT DO YOU ENJOY AT CHURCH?

IS THERE ANYTHING THAT CONFUSES
OR FRUSTRATES YOU AT CHURCH?

MY QUESTION TO YOU,

WHAT DO YOU THINK ABOUT WHAT I WROTE?

DO YOU THINK IT'S IMPORTANT TO ATTEND CHURCH?

WHAT DO YOU ENJOY AT CHURCH?

WHAT DO YOU DO WHEN SOMETHING CONFUSES
OR FRUSTRATES YOU AT CHURCH?

YOU & ME

THE MOST GRATEFUL PERSON WE KNOW

YOU

ME

THE MOST WELCOMING PERSON WE KNOW

YOU

ME

THE GREATEST MODEL OF JESUS WE KNOW

YOU

ME

WE WRITE

YOU & ME

WE FEEL COZY WHEN WE WEAR

YOU

ME

WE FEEL MOST LIKE OURSELVES WHEN WE WEAR

YOU

ME

WE FEEL READY FOR CHURCH WHEN WE WEAR

YOU

ME

DEAR CHILD,

HOW HAVE YOU SEEN GOD'S HAND IN YOUR DAY?

HOW DOES THAT MAKE YOU FEEL?

SHOW ME A PICTURE

MY QUESTION FOR YOU,

HOW HAVE YOU SEEN GOD'S HAND IN YOUR DAY?

HOW DOES THAT MAKE YOU FEEL?

SHOW ME A PICTURE

YOU WRITE

AT EASTER, MY HOUSE

SMELLS LIKE _____

TASTES LIKE _____

LOOKS LIKE _____

SOUNDS LIKE _____

FEELS LIKE _____

MY CHURCH

SMELLS LIKE _____

TASTES LIKE _____

LOOKS LIKE _____

SOUNDS LIKE _____

FEELS LIKE _____

ADULT WRITES

I REALLY LOVE THIS TRADITION

_____

_____

I TRY TO MAKE THE HOLIDAY NICER FOR PEOPLE I
LOVE BY_____

_____

I TRY TO MAKE IT A NICER CELEBRATION FOR THOSE
IN NEED BY_____

_____

I THINK THAT BEING A CHRISTIAN AT EASTER MEANS

_____

_____

MY FAVORITE PART OF THE EASTER STORY IS

_____

_____

I THINK JESUS WAS VERY BRAVE BECAUSE

_____

_____

I WRITE

AT EASTER, MY HOUSE

SMELLS LIKE _____

TASTES LIKE _____

LOOKS LIKE _____

SOUNDS LIKE _____

FEELS LIKE _____

MY CHURCH

SMELLS LIKE _____

TASTES LIKE _____

LOOKS LIKE _____

SOUNDS LIKE _____

FEELS LIKE _____

I REALLY LOVE THIS TRADITION

_____

_____

I TRY TO MAKE THE HOLIDAY NICER FOR PEOPLE I
LOVE BY_____

_____

I TRY TO MAKE IT A NICER CELEBRATION FOR THOSE
IN NEED BY_____

_____

I THINK THAT BEING A CHRISTIAN AT EASTER MEANS

_____

_____

MY FAVORITE PART OF THE EASTER STORY IS

_____

_____

I THINK JESUS WAS VERY BRAVE BECAUSE

_____

_____

I WRITE

RIGHT NOW, I'M PRAYING FOR

THIS ROOM

THIS EVERYDAY OBJECT

THIS EVENT ON THE CALENDAR

THIS PART OF ME

THIS PERSON

THIS _____

RIGHT NOW, I'M PRAYING FOR

YOU WRITE

THIS ROOM

THIS EVERYDAY OBJECT

THIS EVENT ON THE CALENDAR

THIS PART OF ME

THIS PERSON

THIS _____

I WRITE

WAYS I CAN EXPRESS MY LOVE TO GOD WITH MY

MIND

HEART

MOUTH

HANDS

FEET

EARS

EYES

KNEES

ARMS

HOLY BIBLE

DATE

YOU WRITE

WAYS I CAN EXPRESS MY LOVE TO GOD WITH MY

MIND

HEART

MOUTH

HANDS

FEET

EARS

EYES

KNEES

ARMS

DEAR CHILD,

I REALLY ADMIRE YOUR FAITH IN GOD WHEN YOU

1.

2.

3.

I THINK OF YOU WHENEVER

MY QUESTION FOR YOU,

I REALLY ADMIRE YOUR FAITH IN GOD WHEN YOU

1.

2.

3.

I THINK OF YOU WHENEVER

THINGS THAT HAVE BROUGHT US JOY

I WRITE

_____

_____

_____

_____

YOU WRITE

_____

_____

_____

_____

THANK YOU, GOD!

I WRITE

WHEN I GROW OLDER, I REALLY WANT TO

_____

_____

_____

_____

_____

YOU WRITE

MY PRAYER FOR YOU AS YOU GROW OLDER, MY CHILD

_____

_____

_____

_____

_____

DEAR CHILD,

TELL ME HOW CHRIST INSPIRES YOU TO LIVE

IN WHAT WAYS DID HE DEMONSTRATE
LOVE AND KINDNESS TO OTHERS?

HOW DID HE SHOW FORGIVENESS?

LIST A FEW THINGS YOU'VE DONE
LATELY THAT FEEL CHRISTLIKE

1.

2.

CHILD WRITES

HOW IS OUR WORLD A BETTER PLACE
BECAUSE OF CHRIST?

TELL ME ABOUT AN OBSTACLE JESUS HAD TO
OVERCOME. DO YOU THINK YOU COULD DO THAT?

IF YOU COULD MEET JESUS IN PERSON TODAY,
WHAT WOULD YOU WANT TO SAY TO HIM?

MY QUESTION FOR YOU,

TELL ME HOW CHRIST INSPIRES YOU TO LIVE

IN WHAT WAYS DID HE DEMONSTRATE
LOVE AND KINDNESS TO OTHERS?

HOW DID HE SHOW FORGIVENESS?

LIST A FEW THINGS YOU'VE DONE
LATELY THAT FEEL CHRISTLIKE

1.

2.

ADULT WRITES

HOW IS OUR WORLD A BETTER PLACE
BECAUSE OF CHRIST?

TELL ME ABOUT AN OBSTACLE JESUS HAD TO
OVERCOME. DO YOU THINK YOU COULD DO THAT?

IF YOU COULD MEET JESUS IN PERSON TODAY,
WHAT WOULD YOU WANT TO SAY TO HIM?

I WRITE

TODAY I AM GRATEFUL FOR

YOU WRITE

TODAY I AM GRATEFUL FOR

MY QUESTION FOR YOU,

TELL ME ABOUT A RELATIVE OR FRIEND
I DIDN'T GET TO KNOW WELL

DEAR CHILD,

WHY IS PRAYER IMPORTANT TO YOU?

HOW IS PRAYING DIFFICULT FOR YOU?

HOW IS IT EASY?

DO YOU HAVE ANY ADVICE FOR WHEN
PRAYING CAN BE DIFFICULT FOR ME?

WHY IS PRAYER IMPORTANT TO YOU?

HOW IS PRAYING CHALLENGING FOR YOU?
HOW IS IT EASY?

I WRITE

I'M GRATEFUL GOD HAS GIVEN ME YOU BECAUSE

BY KEEPING THIS JOURNAL TOGETHER,
I FEEL LIKE WE

YOU WRITE

DATE

I'M GRATEFUL GOD HAS GIVEN ME YOU BECAUSE

BY KEEPING THIS JOURNAL TOGETHER,
I FEEL LIKE WE

DEAR CHILD,

TELL ME WHAT ELSE IS ON YOUR MIND

YOU & ME

HERE'S A PICTURE OF YOU & ME,
THANKFUL THAT GOD HAS GIVEN US

_____!

YAHOO! WE'VE COMPLETED OUR JOURNAL!
WHAT DID YOU ENJOY ABOUT WRITING TOGETHER?

JOURNALING WITH ONE ANOTHER FELT

HOW SHOULD WE CELEBRATE OUR
JOURNAL'S COMPLETION?

IS THERE A LAST PRAYER WE SHOULD
WRITE IN THIS JOURNAL TOGETHER?

WHAT SHOULD WE DO WITH THIS JOURNAL?